July 18, 1971

For Blanche and Lenny Forest,

With highest regard and much love,

Irma G. Rhodes

IN QUEST OF TREASURE

IN QUEST OF TREASURE

New Poems for Young People

WITH STUDY GUIDES

Irma G. Rhodes

An *Exposition-Banner* Book
Exposition Press   New York

EXPOSITION PRESS INC.

50 Jericho Turnpike   Jericho, New York 11753

FIRST EDITION, SECOND PRINTING

© 1971 by Irma G. Rhodes. *All rights reserved, including the right of reproduction in whole or in part in any form except for short quotations in critical essays and reviews.* Manufactured in the United States of America.

LIBRARY OF CONGRESS CATALOG CARD NUMBER: 79-164866

0-682-47321-9

Contents

PREFACE	7
ACKNOWLEDGMENTS	9
FOREWORD	11
Earthbound	13
Master Scientist	15
Dreams	17
Far Better Truth	19
Metamorphosis	20
The Duck's Boast	22
After the Rain	24
Opposing Viewpoints	25
Security	27
To the Guinea Pig	29
To the White Mouse	31
The Chameleon	33
Museum Piece	35
Early Blossoming	38
Spring Sacrament	40
April Day	41
The Daffodil and the Violet	42
The Lowly Dandelion	44
Dandelion Gone to Seed	45
Triumph of May	47
The Yield	48
Early Autumn	50
Late Autumn	51
Winter Begins	52

February Sunlight	53
March	54
Snow in March	56
The Child-Sculptor	57
To Oberon	59
For Titania	60
The Ocean's Gift	61
Treasure-Trove	63
Argus-Eyed	65
Eyrie	67
Fireworks at Coney Island	68
AFTERWORD	71

Preface

Poetry is for thinking, for feeling, for enjoying—all of which are deeply experienced in reading this book. In my own encounters with these poems I found myself saying, "Yes, that's the way it is." Or sometimes, "That's something I never saw—never understood—never appreciated that way before." The renewal and reinforcement of what is familiar or the eye-opening journey into some unexplored territory of thinking and feeling is the kind of enjoyment to be found here.

The range of subjects is wide, and the modulations of tone extend from the serious to the lighthearted. The sheer beauty and sensitivity of the poems are rare indeed.

Each of us as a human being is a part of all that he has read. The writer influences us, informs or misinforms us, leads or misleads us. To be informed and led by Irma Rhodes is an enriching experience.

JEROME CARLIN
Director of English
New York City Schools

Acknowledgments

I showed several of these poems, which I had been using with good effect in my sophomore English classes at Jamaica High School, to a friend, Mr. Lawrence H. Alexander, Principal of Public School 205, Queens, New York. He asked to see the rest and immediately proposed that I compile them, with study aids, as a textbook for students of the secondary school. My response to his suggestion, for which I am very grateful, is *In Quest of Treasure*.

I am indebted also to Miss Jennifer Craig, Poetry Editor of the Spencer Book Company, Santa Ana, California, whose interest in my work encouraged this undertaking. Four of the poems in this collection, "Earthbound," "Master Scientist," "Metamorphosis" and "The Yield," first appeared in *Poetry Parade*, a quarterly which she edited.

Foreword

Poetry is not a mere ornament of life; it is the substance of life itself. Because I wished my two daughters to grow up with a heightened awareness of the wonder and the beauty of life, I wrote these poems for them during their early school years. It was a mutually rewarding experience, for I recaptured the newness of their vision, while they developed enhanced understanding and appreciation of both poetry and life.

I have now collected these poems for other young people and have supplied study guides to direct their attention primarily to words, ideas and feelings and secondarily to figures of speech, stanza patterns and other techniques of verse, in the hope that they will gain as much pleasure from this project as Enid and Nola did.

The title of the book, *In Quest of Treasure*, reflects my search for life's greatest riches. I have found them in the magnificence of nature, the miracle of human development and the power of poetry. Each reader will pursue his own quest in life. May his rewards be equally soul-satisfying.

IRMA G. RHODES

Earthbound

When spacemen set their beachheads up
On Luna's alabaster shore,
And astrophysicists proclaim
Each pit or peak the crews explore,

I'll stay earthbound. Achilles longed
For helotage on earth instead
Of airless, bloodless, joyless sway
As shadow prince among the dead.

Need I, while yet I draw deep breath,
Forsake the fruitfulness I know
For alabaster sands wherein
Not even asphodel can grow?

STUDY GUIDE

1. In this fantastic age of space travel and moon landings, the writer affirms her love for life on earth. "I'll stay earthbound," she announces in this poem and contrasts the barrenness of the dead planet with the fruitfulness of the living one. This entire volume, in fact, celebrates her joy in life on earth.
2. In the first stanza the moon is given her Latin name, *Luna*. Incidentally, the word *lunatic* is derived from it. At one time it was thought that the moon's influence could injure the mind.
3. *Alabaster* in line 2 is a poetic, not a scientific, description. This mineral is typically white, granular and translucent.

4. Who are astrophysicists? Where do they do their work? Name some of the Apollo crewmen. What explorations have already taken place on the moon?
5. *Achilles,* the great Greek hero of the Trojan War, appears in Book Eleven of *The Odyssey* as a *shadow prince among the dead.* He is wretched in Hades, despite his high position. This son of a king would gladly become a slave on earth, if only he could return to the land of the living. Line 7 explains why.
6. To the author of this poem the moon is more desolate than Hades, for not even the flower of the land of the dead, the *asphodel,* can grow in Luna's *alabaster sands* (lines 11 and 12).
7. How do you feel about travel to the moon and possibilities of future colonization there? Discuss.
8. Master these additional words:
   a. beachheads (line 1)
   b. proclaim (line 3)
   c. earthbound (title and line 5)
   d. helotage (line 6)

Master Scientist

The chemist weaves new fabrics
   Like nylon spun of tars,
The physicist hurls rockets
   To probe the moon and stars,

Geneticists develop
   The strains they choose to grow;
But in which laboratory
   Do the heavens compound snow?

From what unearthly beaker
   Are seas and oceans poured?
In what celestial vessel
   Are springtime magics stored?

What cyclotronic currents
   Unmeasurable by man
Bombarded primal atoms
   When life on earth began?

Study Guide

1. The author pays tribute to the chemist, physicist and geneticist for their modern-day scientific marvels. Then she wonders about the *Master Scientist* who performs the ever-recurring miracles of snow formation, renewal of seas and oceans, and rebirth of nature in the spring. The last stanza asks in scientific terms the ultimate question about how life on earth began. Each reader will answer the questions—or leave them unanswered—

in accordance with his own background. Either way, speculation about these awe-inspiring phenomena adds a new dimension to thinking and feeling.
2. *Scientist* is derived from *scientia*, the Latin word for *knowledge*. Knowledge is power. The Master Scientist, then, has the boundless power (*omnipotence*) conferred by supreme knowledge (*omniscience*). *Omnis* in Latin means *all*.
3. The new man-made fabrics are called *synthetics*. They have remarkable properties, some of them rivaling those of natural materials.
4. What is the meaning of *probe* in line 4? What good has come from this kind of study of the moon and stars?
5. What is a *beaker*? Why does the author speak of an *unearthly* one in line 9?
6. What is meant by *celestial vessel* in line 11? What are some of the *springtime magics* that have enchanted you? Why is the word *stored* used in line 12?
7. What are *cyclotronic currents* (line 13)? From what field is the phrase taken? Why are these currents *unmeasurable by man* (line 14)? What are *primal atoms* (line 15)?

Dreams

Dreams at night
   Come foul or fair,
Shadow-etched
   I know not where;

But daydreams are
   My own design,
Cut with chisel
   Superfine.

STUDY GUIDE

1. Dreams have always been the subject of much speculation and interpretation. Psychologists and psychiatrists often analyze the dreams of patients for clues to their problems.
2. All of us have experienced nighttime *dreams* that are *foul* (*nightmares*) as well as those that are *fair*. Psychologists say the former frequently result from anxiety, and the latter from thoughts of wish-fulfillment. The writer professes ignorance of their source. Note her *metaphor, shadow-etched* (line 3), to describe these dreams. The phrase combines the unreal world of shadows with the real world of the artist who engraves his pictures on a metal plate, just as dreams themselves unite the unreal world with the real one. As you can see from this illustration, a metaphor is an imaginative comparison between ideas not usually associated with each other.

3. The second stanza contrasts *daydreams* with sleep-related dreams. In this passage the metaphor comes from the sculptor's studio. The artist here is awake and is aware of the pattern he chooses to fashion. The *chisel superfine* is used to trace the delicate fantasy of the reverie.

Teachers and parents sometimes rebuke their students and children for daydreaming instead of giving attention. It is a mistake to do so unless the young person habitually lapses into reverie to escape reality. Daydreaming can be a highly creative activity, engaging both the imagination and the intellect, and enabling the dreamer to see new relationships and dimensions and to shape new ideas and worlds.

Far Better Truth

Far better truth from lips that hurt
Than falsehood though it please:
The one a surgeon's cleansing knife;
The other a disease.

STUDY GUIDE

1. The aim of this poem is to teach a lesson. Such verse is called *didactic*.
2. The metaphors in lines 3 and 4 make the message clear, vivid and memorable.
3. Have you experienced the healing power of hearing the truth (or telling it) under painful circumstances? The relief truly resembles that afforded by recovery from surgery. Discuss.
4. Infection caused by a lie can make one as feverish as infection produced by a germ. Explain and illustrate.

Metamorphosis

Do caterpillars' minds comprise
Desire to be butterflies?

Tentacled to earthbound things
Before they know release of wings,

Are they content with groveling,
With many-footed traveling,

Because they do not realize
Their true domain is in the skies?

Or does anticipated bliss
Of future metamorphosis

Teach them to wait with confidence
For their assured inheritance?

Study Guide

1. The word *metamorphosis* is a term you may have studied in your science courses. It means a *change of form* and is used for such developments as the transformation of the caterpillar into the butterfly and of the tadpole into the frog.
2. *Personification* gives the poem its form, substance and spirit. This device endows abstractions, inanimate things and creatures other than man with human characteristics. Like all figures, it makes ideas lively and picturesque.

3. What is the effect of the question technique throughout the poem? Even if there are no sure answers, what value is derived from considering possibilities?
4. What does the phrase *release of wings* (line 4) mean? For centuries man sought this kind of release. Now at last he has perfected planes and rockets to such a degree that he is no longer earthbound.
5. Why is the caterpillars' system of locomotion called *groveling* (line 5)?
6. What is meant by the caterpillars' *true domain* (line 8)? What is man's true domain: the earth, the moon or Mars? Discuss.
7. What does *anticipated bliss* (line 9) mean?
8. Waiting may be easy for caterpillars. For human beings —especially children—it is often very hard. Young people are impatient to grow up, for instance, even though maturation to adulthood is an *assured inheritance* (line 12). It is important to accept each stage of life not merely with patience, but with gladness.
9. Look up these words in the dictionary:
a. comprise (line 1)
b. tentacled (line 3)
c. anticipated (line 9)

The Duck's Boast

I am equally at home
On land, at sea, in sky.
Though I roost with barnyard folk
Not so versatile as I,
My dreams are not of coops
And slops, like theirs.

I have felt the vibrant air
Uphold my circling wings;
I can somersault to fish
For underwater things;
I dream of coral reefs
And clouds like stairs.

Study Guide

1. In the first stanza, while the duck speaks boastfully of himself and contemptuously of the other barnyard creatures, he does not antagonize the reader. Truth, after all, is his defense. Furthermore, he is speaking for all ducks, not for himself alone. Support the truth of his assertions in these first six lines.
2. Having established his claim, he no longer needs to make invidious comparisons with his inferiors. In stanza 2 he is content to describe his skills and his aspirations.
3. Note the rhyme scheme and the pleasure it affords.
4. Lines 6 and 12 have only two stresses instead of three. What is the effect of this change?
5. A *simile* occurs in the last line (*clouds like stairs*).

This figure presents an imaginative comparison introduced by either *like* or *as*.
6. Master these words:
   a. versatile (line 4)
   b. vibrant (line 7)
   c. coral (line 11)

After the Rain

Transmuted is
   The garden now:
Rare emeralds gem
   Each leafy bough;

On every rose
   A diamond crown
Illuminates
   Her velvet gown;

And birds of jet
   In fonts of pearl
Baptize themselves
   With raindrop-swirl.

STUDY GUIDE

1. The writer observes the transformation of the garden by the miracle of rain. Note what happens to the leaves, the roses, the birds and the bird baths.
2. The figure of speech used conspicuously in this poem is the metaphor. Like the simile, it presents an imaginative comparison, but it omits the introductory *like* or *as*. Thus, the leaves after the rain are described as gemmed with *emeralds* (line 3). Select the other metaphors in the poem.
3. In the third stanza, which draws upon the baptismal ceremony for its imagery, personification is used. What is the effect of this figure?
4. Add the following words to your vocabulary:
    a. transmuted (line 1)
    b. illuminates (line 7)
    c. fonts (line 10)

Opposing Viewpoints

I—Ours

Amber wears a collar now,
    Studded with a silver bell,
Token of our ownership
    Of the kitten nonpareil.
How we love the tinkling sound
Telling us our pet's around!

II—Amber's

This that jangles at my throat
    Strangles feline enterprise!
Stalking's now a vain pretense:
    Leper-like, I must advise
Every apprehensive ear
Whether I am far or near.

Study Guide

Note

    The two viewpoints expressed here show that there are gaps in understanding between pets and their loving owners, just as there are gaps in understanding between children and their loving parents. It is important to develop interest in the ideas of others. Increased tolerance will come with greater awareness of what those with whom you associate are thinking and feeling.

I

1. What does the collar symbolize to the family?
2. What word especially shows the great pride the family members take in their pet? What does it mean? Look up its derivation.
3. What comfort do these people derive from the *tinkling sound* (line 5) of the bell?

II

1. Amber's strong dislike of the bell is conveyed in the first line by the word *jangles*. Contrast this term with the one used by the family for the very same sound. To emphasize his feeling, Amber employs *internal rhyme*. *Strangles* in the second line not only matches *jangles* in sound, but it also agrees with it in emotional tone. Both words produce decidedly unpleasant sensations.
2. Explain *feline enterprise* (line 2) and *stalking* (line 3). Why does a well-fed domestic animal continue to be interested in prey? What is the term for this pattern of behavior?
3. Explain the reference in the expression *leper-like* in line 4. Where have you read about the ancient treatment of lepers? How are these unfortunates cared for today?
4. Explain *apprehensive ear* in line 5. Which creatures would appreciate the warning sounded by the bell?

Security

The tortoise occupies, rent-free,
  A sturdy house of horn:
What men must toil a lifetime for
  Is his before he's born.

You'd think he'd be a reveler,
  Secure from fortune's blows;
Yet this unmortgaged fellow is
  Afraid to poke his nose

Beyond his overlapping eaves—
  His thrust of limb and mind
Conditioned by the residence
  He cannot leave behind.

STUDY GUIDE

1. Generally *security* is regarded as a very desirable thing, and it usually is. Parents strive to give their children emotional and financial security, for example. Here, however, it proves to be less than a blessing. An excess of a virtue may become a vice. Thus, overprotection inhibits the tortoise, instead of freeing him. Can this observation apply to people also? Discuss.
2. What figure of speech is used all through the poem? What does it contribute to the thought, feeling and tone of the piece?
3. What is meant by the tortoise's *house of horn* (line 2)? In what sense is it a house? Why is the tortoise con-

sidered *unmortgaged* (line 7)? What are his *overlapping eaves* (line 9)?
4. In the last three lines freedom of movement and freedom of mind are linked. Is this true of people as well as of tortoises? Discuss.

Here is another point to ponder: how much freedom of action and of thought should people—especially young people—be given? Are there any limits to liberty? Can one person's liberty ever encroach upon that of others? Consider carefully.
5. Study these words:
   a. security (title)
   b. reveler (line 5)
   c. conditioned (line 11)

To the Guinea Pig

I salute you, guinea pig,
Member of a martyr race;
The crown of thorns upon your brow
Endows you with a special grace.

Not clever like your cousin rat,
Nor pretty like albino mice,
You yet surpass this fellowship
In patience and self-sacrifice.

Small actor of heroic role,
You do not posture, rant or rage,
But munch your shredded escarole
Till curtain time upon your stage.

STUDY GUIDE

1. This poem pays tribute to one of the unsung heroes of science, the *guinea pig*, used for experimental purposes in the laboratory. What does the crown of thorns symbolize?
2. The guinea pig is a rodent, like his *cousin rat* (line 5), but he is a simpler creature. What are *albino mice* (line 6)? What makes them pretty? What special virtues does the guinea pig have that compensate for his lack of cleverness and beauty?
3. Personification is the figure employed throughout the poem. In the last stanza this figure produces a combination of pathos and humor through the use of terms

from the world of the theater. Show how this is accomplished.
4. Master these words:
   a. martyr (line 2)
   b. surpass (line 7)
   c. posture (line 10)
   d. rant (line 10)
   e. escarole (line 11)
   f. curtain time (line 12)

To the White Mouse

Arrayed in royal ermine,
   Aristocratic mouse,
As far removed from vermin
   As palace is from house!

The palace you inhabit,
   A laboratory maze—
To guinea pig and rabbit
   And you, my song of praise!

Although you look too fragile
   For martyrdom's hard role,
Your limbs and nerves prove agile,
   And durable your soul.

So here's to you in ermine,
   Of mice aristocrat,
While scientists determine
   Your ergs and things like that!

STUDY GUIDE

1. What is *ermine*? Why is it described as *royal* (line 1)? Why is the white mouse said to be *aristocratic* (line 2)?
2. What is a *laboratory maze* (line 6)? What kind of testing utilizes this device?
3. Personification, used in the entire poem, is particularly poignant in the third stanza. Which word in this division is the ultimate tribute to the human-like qualities of the white mouse? Explain.

4. What is the literal meaning of *ergs* (line 16)? How is the term used here?
5. You have probably noticed the rhymes: *ermine, vermin; inhabit, rabbit; fragile, agile; ermine, determine.* They give double pleasure, because in each case, the last *two* syllables rhyme. Appropriately enough, this is called *double rhyme.*
6. Study the following words:
   a. vermin (line 3)
   b. agile (line 11)
   c. durable (line 12)
   d. ergs (line 16)

The Chameleon

Now we see you; now we don't:
   Conjurer of inborn skill.
Tell us, please, chameleon,
   How you blush and blanch at will.

Frailest of an ancient stock,
   Dragon-race that men abhor,
Who'd have thought by wizardry
   You'd outlive tyrannosaur?

STUDY GUIDE

1. The *chameleon* is a dainty little lizard with the highly developed power of changing the color of its skin. This phenomenon is known as *protective coloration*, a survival technique, and the innate pattern of behavior that produces it is called a *reflex*.
2. The chameleon is addressed directly, not spoken of indirectly. What is the effect of this device?
3. Why is the small creature called a *conjurer* in line 2? This is an instance of personification, as you will readily recognize.
4. Another poetic device found in this poem is *alliteration*, the use of the same initial sound in two or more words in a group. Note its occurrence in the phrase *blush and blanch*. What colors do these words suggest?
5. What is meant by *dragon-race* in line 6? The word *abhor* is a strong term. By derivation it means to *shrink with horror from* something repugnant. Why is it appropriate in this line?

6. What is the meaning of *wizardry* in line 7? Is it used literally or figuratively? Explain. To what term in stanza 1 is it related?
7. *Tyrannosaur* was the largest carnivorous dinosaur. It measured about forty-seven feet in length. Even its skeletal remains look terrifying.
8. The question with which the poem closes should make you reflect about the qualities that determine survival of any species. Are huge bulk and ferocious appearance guarantees of the perpetuation of an individual or a group? The destruction of giants by little men is a familiar and gratifying theme in literature. Can you think of any examples? Perhaps a famous Bible story comes to mind in this connection. You may also know Homer's version of Odysseus' encounter with the Cyclops Polyphemus. And, of course, a popular fairy tale will undoubtedly occur to you.

Museum Piece

Behold tyrannosaur,
Restored by fossil-lore:

He must have been a sight
To freeze the blood with fright

When flesh was on those bones,
Now dry and hard as stones.

That dagger-studded jaw
Appeased his greedy maw;

He snorted blue-green fire;
His bloodshot eyes flashed ire;

His voice, a thunderous roar
On Mesozoic shore,

Made every living thing
Abominate the king

Of dinosaurs. Once more
Observe tyrannosaur:

The specimen above
Can't scare a turtledove!

STUDY GUIDE

1. *Tyrannosaur* is familiar to you from his appearance in "The Chameleon" (page 33). His name, from the Greek, literally means *despot-lizard*. Here he is on display in a

museum, his bones wired together by *fossil* experts. When you study geology, you will be fascinated by the ingenuity of these scientific sleuths who reconstruct the prehistoric past of the earth from any remains, such as animal bones or even leaf imprints, of previous ages.
2. The writer, viewing the skeleton of tyrannosaur, readily imagines what he looked like in the flesh and surmises the terror he must have inspired.
3. What figure of speech is used in *dagger-studded jaw* (line 7)?
4. What is the effect of his snorting *blue-green fire* (line 9)? Of his *bloodshot eyes* (line 10)? Of the *thunderous roar* of his voice (line 11)? What senses are aroused by these descriptions?
5. *Mesozoic* (line 12) is the name of the geological age of reptiles.
6. *Dinosaur*, like *tyrannosaur*, is also derived from the Greek. It means *terrible lizard*.
7. In the first two lines of the poem the writer acts as a museum guide, calling attention to an interesting exhibit. Then her imagination reconstructs a now-extinct specimen of ancient horror. After picturing him, with sound effects, as if he were still alive, she returns to where she started from: the display case of the museum. This time reflection supersedes imagination as she is struck by the supreme irony that the former tyrant now cannot frighten even *a turtledove*, a bird so gentle that its family is used as the symbol of peace.

There is a Latin proverb *Sic semper tyrannis,* the motto of the state of Virginia, that comes to mind in this connection. A literal translation of this saying is: *Thus always to tyrants.* This is a comforting thought; but even if they are deposed in the end, despots have

throughout history destroyed human lives, achievements and aspirations. Can you cite any examples of such tyranny, past or present?
8. Master these words:
   a. restored (line 2)
   b. fossil-lore (line 2)
   c. appeased (line 8)
   d. maw (line 8)
   e. ire (line 10)
   f. abominate (line 14)

Early Blossoming

Persuaded by untimely warmth
    To early blossoming,
Magnolia trees performed the rites
    Initiating spring.

Each happy fur-clad floweret
    Stripped off its winter coat
To flaunt a velvet ball gown worth
    A famed couturier's note.

The north wind disapproved of this
    Presumptuous display
And cooled the ardor of the spring
    With breath that brought dismay.

The unprotected blossoms winced
    As winter violence tore
Their finery inadequate
    To brave the frost once more.

And though the spring is certain now,
    Alas, not sun nor rain
Can mend or patch or starch or press
    Their tattered clothes again.

Study Guide

1. While winter with its rigors drags on, everyone yearns for the coming of spring. A premature blossoming, however, can be disastrous, as this poem observes. Have

you heard the expression: "Everything in due time"? Patience is not only a great virtue; it is also a sound philosophy by which one can live.
2. Notice the word *rites* in line 3. It is a religious term, appropriate to the season. Many religions of ancient origin celebrate the return of spring as a time of rebirth, physical and spiritual. Do you know Stravinsky's deeply moving *Rite of Spring*?
3. Throughout the poem personification is used. It contributes vividness, as you have come to expect; but it also adds pathos here, for the reader can empathize with the sufferings of the trees. Select every instance of this figure that you can find.
4. Observe the stanza form. It is determined by the number of lines, the number of stresses in each line (that is, the rhythm) and the rhyme pattern. This is the famous ballad stanza, simple and singable.
5. Master these additional words:
   a. initiating (line 4)
   b. flaunt (line 7)
   c. couturier's (line 8)
   d. presumptuous (line 10)
   e. ardor (line 11)
   f. inadequate (line 15)

Spring Sacrament

The cherry tree is a bride white-clad;
   Her bridesmaid in pink, the peach;
And bridal wreath festoons the hall
   Where April, the pastor, will preach;

Bird-song is the orchestra;
   But who is the chosen groom?
Will he come as the sun, the wind or the rain
   To this holy place in bloom?

Study Guide

1. The glory of early spring is presented in terms of the rite of marriage. What is the figure used throughout?
2. Several examples of alliteration are found here. Note its use in line 2 (*pink . . . peach*) and in line 4 (*pastor . . . preach*). The title is also alliterative.
3. What is the effect of the question with which the poem ends? Are all three natural forces possible grooms? If so, in what sense?
4. In what respects may any orchard at any time be regarded as a *holy place?*
5. What is the stanza form employed here?
6. Master the words below:
    a. sacrament (title)
    b. festoons (line 3)
    c. pastor (line 4)

April Day

She teases with bright sun of June;
Then freezes with March winds by noon;

Just now she feigned November's gloom—
And yet the jonquils dare to bloom!

Study Guide

1. As this poem observes, an April day has many moods, some of them bleak. Despite her seeming contrariness, however, she does not intimidate the jonquils. How do they know their time to bloom has come?
2. Note the internal rhyme in *teases* and *freezes*. The rhyme is double, as well, for both syllables of both words match.
3. What figure of speech appears in lines 1, 3 and 4?

The Daffodil and the Violet

The daffodil in stiff-necked pride
Emblazons all the countryside;
The violet crouches, quite unseen,
Within the shelter of her green.

But tested in a sudden squall,
The daffodil is the one to fall;
For pride is not so strong a stuff
As modesty, when winds blow rough.

Study Guide

1. Which of these two flowers does the writer seem to prefer? Why? Do you share her preference? Why or why not?
2. Note the figure of speech in *stiff-necked pride* (line 1). What does its use contribute to the thought and feeling of the poem?
3. *Emblazons* (line 2) is a term from heraldry. Check the meaning in the dictionary.
4. Pride may be a virtue or a vice, depending upon its kind and degree. It is used in a favorable sense in the expression "pride in one's work." In line 7 of this poem, however, the implication is unfavorable; as it is, also, in the often-quoted "Pride goeth before destruction. . . ." The ancient Greeks looked upon excessive pride, which they called *hubris,* as sinful. Their tragic heroes were afflicted with this flaw in character.
5. The conclusion drawn in the last two lines is known as

a *moral*. Is it a valid observation about life? Explain and illustrate from your experience or reading.
6. Notice the rhyme pattern. What are some of the values of the use of rhyme?
7. Look up these additional words:
   a. crouches (line 3)
   b. squall (line 5)
   c. modesty (line 8)

The Lowly Dandelion

I love the lowly dandelion
The gardener calls a weed;
Its golden rays outshine the blaze
Of flowers pedigreed.

It thrives in dust as well as loam,
In scorching heat or cold;
It turns the other cheek to wrath
As if it had been told.

Study Guide

1. Once again the writer extols the modest, the humble, the meek. What superiority does she claim for the *lowly dandelion* in the first stanza? Do you share her enthusiasm for this flower? Why or why not?
2. What virtue of the dandelion does she celebrate in the second stanza? With what effect does she use personification in the last two lines?
3. Note that in line 3 *rays* rhymes with *blaze*. This is another example of internal rhyme.
4. Learn the following words:
   a. pedigreed (line 4)
   b. loam (line 5)
   c. wrath (line 7)

Dandelion Gone to Seed

The iris dead upon its stalk
    Is symbol of despair;
Its blackened petals mortify
    The flesh that was so fair.

The lily of the valley shines
    And shrivels in a day;
Its brittle bells pronounce the knell
    Of imminent decay.

But dandelion gone to seed
    Is daintier than in bloom:
A hundred feathered arrowlets
    Bear hope instead of gloom!

STUDY GUIDE

1. This little poem is concerned with two of the eternal themes of man's experience and his quest for knowledge: death and survival. Science, psychology, philosophy and religion have all participated in this great search for understanding. The author does not pretend to make a contribution to any of the aforementioned areas; she merely observes and reflects upon the death of three of her best-loved flowers.
2. The first stanza comments on the sad spectacle of the dead *iris*. No hint of the living beauty that gave it its name (from *Iris*, the ancient Greek goddess of the rainbow) remains. *Mortify* in line 3 means *humiliate*. Interestingly enough, it is derived from the Latin word for death, *mors*. What is the figure of speech in line 4?

3. Stanza 2 laments the short life span of the *lily of the valley* and its withered appearance in death. Note the use of alliteration in lines 5, 6 and 7.
4. Stanza 3 contrasts the transfiguration of the *dandelion* in death with the deterioration of both the iris and the lily of the valley in the same state. The dandelion's physical glorification delights the eye, but what delights the heart is the promise of survival through the *hundred feathered arrowlets*. The perpetuation of life itself is celebrated here.
5. Define:
   a. knell (line 7)
   b. imminent (line 8)
   c. arrowlets (line 11)
6. On the subject of survival, compare the implications of this poem with those suggested by "The Chameleon" (page 33).

Triumph of May

A dank and dismal April
Ended yesterday
With incandescent sunshine
Inaugurating May.

Forgotten winter's conquest,
Early spring's retreat;
Though late, the final triumph
Obliterates defeat.

Study Guide

1. There are two instances of alliteration in the first stanza. Select them and comment upon their effect.
2. Spring is sometimes fickle. Though she is expected on March 21, she may delay her arrival by weeks. This poem describes such a belated season. April has been guilty of defection, but May has made reparation.
3. In the second stanza the terms are all borrowed from the military: *conquest, retreat, triumph, defeat.* What is the name of the figure of speech they exemplify?
4. The last two lines express a philosophy that applies to life generally. In all areas of human concern, there may be delays, discouragements, reverses, failures. Patience, faith and courage will enable an individual, a group, a race, a nation and the world to persist until *the final triumph obliterates defeat.* Illustrate the truth of this observation from your experience or reading.
5. Do you know the following words?
    a. dank (line 1)
    b. incandescent (line 3)
    c. inaugurating (line 4)
    d. obliterates (line 8)

The Yield

It was a seed of unknown worth
I planted, for I was not told
If there would issue from the earth
Rank weed or wheat or flower of gold.

I watered it with sweat and tears,
With tears of joy and tears of woe;
I sheltered it against my fears
Of wind and frost and hail and snow.

It grew, and with it grew my need
To know the yield. Each tasseled cane,
As tough and wilful as a weed,
Is burgeoning with bloom and grain!

STUDY GUIDE

1. *Seed* in line 1 may be interpreted literally, as the kernel of a plant sown in the earth. In this case, the meaning of the poem is transparently clear. The word *seed*, however, may be used figuratively of anything that germinates and bears fruit. Thus, it may represent an idea that is propagated—or even a child. In all these instances, the new life will develop only if tended faithfully. And not until the plant matures will the grower know the yield.
2. In the first stanza, if the seed represents an idea or a child, how would you interpret *weed or wheat or flower of gold?*
3. In the second stanza, notice the work, suffering and

fear involved in nurturing a growing thing. What would *wind and frost and hail and snow* represent in the figurative interpretation of the seed?
4. The final stanza expresses a joyous fulfillment, for the plant bears *bloom and grain*. Interpret this rich *yield* in terms of an idea or of a child. Note that suspense has been maintained until the very last line.
5. Study the rhyme scheme. What figure of speech is used in lines 10 and 11? Alliteration appears in lines 11 and 12. Select the two examples.
6. Be sure you understand these words:
   a. rank (line 4)
   b. tasseled (line 10)
   c. cane (line 10)
   d. wilful (line 11)
   e. burgeoning (line 12)

Early Autumn

Asters blue and yellow,
Oak leaves red as rust,
Maple trees all golden,
Earth as dry as dust;

Grapes upon the arbor,
Apples on the bough,
Peach jam in the larder—
Autumn's with us now.

Study Guide

1. Note the emphasis on color in the first three lines. Early autumn is the season richest in jewel-like hues. A drive in the country at this time is a dazzling experience.
2. The theme of the second stanza is the blessing of nature's bounty at harvest time. What religious festivals mark the ingathering of the crops? How are these holidays celebrated?
3. How does the stanza pattern of this poem differ from that of the ballad? How many accented syllables are there in each line? How many unaccented ones?

Late Autumn

Birds are swarming,
Southward bound;
Bruised fruits rot
Upon the ground.

Leaves come swirling
Round and round;
Strong gusts pile them
Mound on mound.

STUDY GUIDE

1. This is a companion piece to "Early Autumn," but what a contrast it presents! Select the details that make the scene dull and desolate.
2. What mood is created? Compare it with the mood established in "Early Autumn."
3. Note that the four words that rhyme—*bound, ground, round* and *mound*—repeat the same note. This is intentional. It suggests the monotony of the late autumn landscape.
4. Master the following words:
   a. swirling (line 5)
   b. mound (line 8)

Winter Begins

Rime on the morning grass,
  Frost on the northern pane,
Snow in the lowering clouds:
  Winter begins his reign.

STUDY GUIDE

1. The signs of winter—*rime, frost* and *snow*—are welcome to skiing enthusiasts and their ilk. They find winter's reign gracious and his season a carnival time. To less hardy folk, like the author, King Winter is a tyrant. The poem is deliberately noncommittal. Discuss it in accordance with your own ideas and feelings.
2. Look up the meaning of *rime* in line 1. Do not confuse it with the variant of *rhyme*.

February Sunlight

February sunlight
With its mighty thrust
Penetrates so deeply
Beneath earth's frozen crust

That every seed or rootlet,
Long buried in the tomb,
Feels the prodding impulse
Toward reviving bloom.

Study Guide

1. Though February is still very much a part of the winter scene with snow, sleet and freezing temperatures, somehow it has an altered look because the sun's rays, being more direct, are brighter. Plants dormant in the earth respond to this change even more readily than people do.
2. Death is associated with winter; resurrection with spring. Note the use of *buried* and *tomb* in line 6 and of *reviving* in line 8.
3. Add the following words to your vocabulary:
   a. penetrates (line 3)
   b. prodding (line 7)
   c. impulse (line 7)

March

March breathes the wrath of winter
   With the friendly smile of spring:
He's so full of contradiction
   That I pity him, poor thing.

I'm certain he's much prouder
   Of the crocus than he shows,
And ashamed of rampant rivers
   Overcharged with melting snows;

But he blusters like a bully
   In an unrepentant mood,
And does everything he shouldn't—
   Though he'd rather, far, be good.

Study Guide

1. Personification is the mind, heart and soul of this poem. Observe its use in each stanza.
2. In the first four lines note that March is regarded with sympathetic understanding of his inconsistency. While his breath is cold, his smile is warm. Explain the *wrath of winter* and the *friendly smile of spring*.
3. The second stanza treats of two conspicuous performances of March, one creative and the other destructive. What are they? What feelings does the author impute to him for each of these activities?
4. The final stanza uses a comparison that combines pathos, humor and psychological insight. Show in detail how this is accomplished.

5. There are several instances of alliteration in the poem. Cite as many as you can.
6. Study the following words:
   a. rampant (line 7)
   b. overcharged (line 8)
   c. blusters (line 9)
   d. unrepentant (line 10)

Snow in March

December snow is a proper thing,
But snow in March is a trespassing;

For winter has no lawful right
Thus to extend his lease by might,

Compelling spring and her retinue
To plead for tenure overdue.

STUDY GUIDE

1. The language of this poem is borrowed from the field of law. What is the effect of such legal terms as *trespassing, lease, plead* and *tenure* in this context? Define each of these words. What figure of speech is involved in their use here?
2. Explain the meaning of spring's *retinue* (line 5). What would you include among these retainers?
3. What is meant by *tenure overdue* (line 6)?
4. What is the tone of the complaint? Is it justified?

The Child-Sculptor

A worn-down broom his only armature,
The rapt child-sculptor overlays the spine
With stuff like Parian: as white, as pure,
As dazzling in the sun, as crystalline;

As cold as marble, too—but at the touch
Of those small hands, it quickens to his will,
Made plastic by the ardor of the clutch
With which he shapes his snowman on the hill.

Study Guide

1. Heaps of snow are as irresistible to the child-sculptor as mounds of clay are to the professional sculptor. Both work with the same impassioned creativeness, though the skills, the materials and, of course, the results are different.
2. The word *armature* is a technical term. It is the name of the framework that supports the clay or wax (or, as here, the snow) used in modeling. What word in the first stanza is a synonym for *armature*?
3. The sculptors of ancient Greece prized *Parian* marble (from the island of Paros) above all other varieties.
4. The word *quickens* in line 6 means *comes to life*.
5. What is the meaning of *plastic* in line 7? The word *ardor* suggests warmth (it is derived from the Latin word meaning *to burn*).
6. Note that each line has five stressed syllables. What is the effect of the longer line, as compared with the lines of three and four stresses in the other poems?

7. Add these words to your active vocabulary:
   a. rapt (line 2)
   b. overlays (line 2)
   c. crystalline (line 4)

To Oberon

I'll wear a veil of Queen Anne's lace
And a coronet of dew,
Beaded by frost and lustered by moon,
The night I marry you;

And on my trembling finger you'll place
A circlet of star-gemmed light,
Token that heaven and earth rejoice
When faithful hearts unite.

Study Guide

1. Oberon and Titania are the king and queen of the fairies in Shakespeare's *A Midsummer Night's Dream.* Here Titania addresses a love poem to her future husband.
2. Are you familiar with the delicate wildflower called Queen Anne's lace? Since fairy folk are associated with the world of nature, a flower-lace veil is suitable for the bride. It is held in place by a crown that resembles pearls in the world of human beings. How do you know from lines 2 and 3 that the coronet is pearl-like?
3. Why is the bride's finger described as *trembling* in line 5?
4. Why is the wedding ring in line 6 called *a circlet of star-gemmed light* instead of a band of diamonds, which it resembles?
5. How do the last two lines apply to the marriage of real people as well as to the union of Oberon and Titania?
6. What stanza form do you recognize here?
7. Master the words below:
    a. lustered (line 3)
    b. circlet (line 6)

For Titania

I'll build you a castle of acorn planks,
    Sawed to expose the vein;
Pave it with blocks of butterfly dust
    And glass it with crystals of rain.

All night you may gambol in glen and in glade,
    But when Lucifer lightens the sky,
And Chanticleer crows his first alarm—
    To your lord and your fortress, fly!

Study Guide

1. Oberon writes this poem for Titania in answer to hers. In what respects does he sound like a human husband?
2. The first stanza suggests the tiny size and fanciful nature of fairy folk. How? What is the effect of the phrase *acorn planks* (line 1)? What would be the equivalent in the real world of *blocks of butterfly dust* (line 3) and of *crystals of rain* (line 4)?
3. Note the use of alliteration in lines 3, 5, 6 and 8.
4. *Lucifer*, which literally means *light-bearer*, is a name for the morning star.
5. Who is *Chanticleer?* What does his name mean?
6. Compare the feminine qualities of Titania's "To Oberon" with the masculine ones of this poem.
7. Master the following words:
   a. gambol (line 5)
   b. glen (line 5)
   c. glade (line 5)

The Ocean's Gift

Selene with her silver wand
　In deft maestro's hand
Bids the mounting seas pour out
　Crescendos on the sand.

On such a shore Demosthenes
　In humbleness and pride
Pitted mortal voice and will
　Against immortal tide.

And though with downbeat of baton
　The goddess might have shown
Demosthenes the emptiness
　Of breath that men intone;

Amazed to find in little man
　A spirit so immense,
She granted him the ocean's gift
　Of silver eloquence.

STUDY GUIDE

1. This poem was suggested by the mythology and history of ancient Greece. It tells the story of Demosthenes, who as a youth suffered from halting speech. To overcome this affliction, he is said to have practiced declamation on the shore of the sea, speaking with a mouth full of pebbles. In this way he overcame the double impediment—the natural one of his tongue and the artificial one of the pebbles—to become the most famous orator

of his country, able to be heard above the roar of the waves or the din of his audiences. Here *Selene*, the Greek goddess of the moon, counterpart of the Roman *Luna*, is said to have granted him this great gift of eloquence.

2. Why is Selene's wand *silver?* She is portrayed in the first stanza as the conductor of an orchestra, with the waves as the musicians that perform according to her directions. What natural phenomenon does this use of personification represent?

3. When Demosthenes appears at the seashore to perfect his speech, he becomes an object of interest to Selene. Explain how he can possess two seemingly incompatible qualities like *humbleness* and *pride* (line 6). Note the use of another contrast in lines 7 and 8.

4. What does *downbeat of baton* in line 9 suggest? What might Selene have done if Demosthenes had displeased her? Explain the *emptiness* of men's breath (lines 11 and 12).

5. Why is man called *little* in line 13? How did Selene react to Demosthenes' greatness of soul? Why is his new power of speech called *the ocean's gift* in line 15? The use of *silver* to describe eloquence alludes to Selene's role in Demosthenes' achievement. Furthermore, it suggests the familiar phrase "the silver-tongued orator." And perhaps it recalls the maxim "Speech is silver; silence, golden."

6. Master these words:
   a. deft (line 2)
   b. maestro's (line 2)
   c. crescendos (line 4)
   d. intone (line 12)

Treasure-Trove

An oyster shell would seem the mine
   Unlikeliest to yield
Such treasure as the regal pearl
   Within its womb congealed.

A dark and stagnant pool you'd think
   Infertile as despair;
Yet that is where the lily grows
   So fragrant and so fair.

Thus, irritation and decay
   Are nature's drill and bit
To sculpture out of finite pain
   Delight that's infinite.

STUDY GUIDE

1. What is the meaning of the title? How can it be applied to the pearl and the lily? What do these two have in common?
2. Why is the oyster shell called a *mine* in line 1? Why is it considered so unlikely to produce treasure? Why is the pearl described as *regal* in line 3? Note the phrase *within its womb congealed* in line 4. Comment on its appropriateness to describe the growth of the pearl. In addition to alliteration, what other figure does it exemplify?
3. The phrase *infertile as despair* in line 6 combines the simile with personification. What makes the compari-

son particularly unusual? Why is despair regarded as infertile? How, then, would you describe hope?

4. To what process does *irritation* in line 9 refer? What is alluded to in *decay* in the same line? Both of these words generally have destructive implications; here, however, they clearly have creative ones. They are presented as nature's tools for the shaping of two objects of surpassing loveliness, the pearl and the lily. The language is borrowed from the sculptor's studio. What is the figure that results? What does *finite pain* in line 11 mean? How does it lead to and enhance the *delight that's infinite* in the last line of the poem?

5. Master the following words:
a. congealed (line 4)
b. stagnant (line 5)

Argus-Eyed

You do not need the hundred eyes
Unsleeping Argus had. For scope
Your two will serve. They sweep the skies
Like Jupiter's, or scrutinize
A germ-bud through a microscope.

Because his eyes did not avail,
Poor Argus lost his fifty pairs,
Which now begem the peacock's tail,
Mere ornaments—like eyes that fail
To see earth's wonders or its snares.

Study Guide

1. Do you know the story of Argus in Greek and Roman mythology? This giant with a hundred eyes was assigned by Juno to guard Io, who was the rival for her husband's affections. When Mercury, sent by Jupiter, lulled Argus to sleep and then killed him, Juno immortalized the giant's eyes in the tail of the peacock, the bird sacred to her.
2. Jupiter, the mighty god of the heavens in ancient Roman religion, could easily scan both sky and earth.
3. According to the author, if you use your two eyes properly, they will enable you to see vast panoramas or to make the most minutely detailed observations of microscopic matter. How can you train your eyes to serve you well?
4. When are eyes *mere ornaments* (line 9)? What loss results? What dangers may be encountered?

5. Plot the rhyme scheme.
6. Master the following words:
   a. scope (line 2)
   b. scrutinize (line 4)
   c. avail (line 6)
   d. begem (line 8)
   e. snares (line 10)

Eyrie

Mountaineers are always free.
Spurning frail security,
They climb the mountain's spiral stair
Step by step to freer air.

As the eagle to the wren,
They leave the vale to lesser men;
Scale the angled crag to find
Eyrie for the dauntless mind.

STUDY GUIDE

1. The opening line is a literal translation of the well-known Latin saying *Montani semper liberi,* used by the state of West Virginia as its motto.
2. Note the phrase *frail security* (line 2), in which the terms are seemingly incongruous. In what sense may security be regarded as unsure? What may be the result of overconfidence that one is safe? Such a use of contradictory terms is the figure known as *oxymoron*.
3. *Spiral stair* in line 3 combines metaphor with alliteration. Why is the mountain path described in this way?
4. What does the *eagle* represent in this poem? What does the *wren* symbolize? Why are these figures particularly appropriate?
5. There is internal rhyme in lines 6 and 7. Select the words involved.
6. Note the phrase *angled crag* in line 7. What does it mean? Observe that the harshness of the sound suits the ruggedness of the scene.
7. Define the title word. What is the meaning of *eyrie for the dauntless mind* (line 8)?

Fireworks at Coney Island

Thunder booms, and stars flower.
The crowd gasps at man's power
To fire the skies. A breathless hour

Man-made planets twink and twirl,
And artificial comets purl;
Then darkness settles in a whirl.

The throng abandons Coney's strand,
For Hesperus is not so grand
As rocket light. Why stare at sand?

Study Guide

1. At New York's famous Coney Island, fireworks displays are not limited to Fourth of July celebrations; they are a weekly attraction throughout the summer season. Here the author records her impression of one such exhibition.
2. In the first stanza note the words and phrases that stimulate the senses of hearing and sight. *Thunder booms*, for example, appeals to the ear, and *stars flower* to the eye. What word in line 2 does the listener hear? In line 3 *fire the skies* makes the reader see a picture and even feel a suggestion of warmth.
3. What senses are affected by *planets twink and twirl* (line 4)? By *comets purl* (line 5)? By *darkness* and *whirl* (line 6)?
4. *Hesperus* (line 8) is the name of the evening star.

5. The poem is written, ostensibly, from the point of view of the crowd. Observe the breathless excitement generated by *man's power* (line 2), *man-made planets* (line 4) and *artificial comets* (line 5). In the third stanza the audience leaves when the show is over because the evening star does not put on such a brilliant performance as man's pyrotechnics do. The question with which the poem ends reflects the mind and mood of the departing throng.
6. Though the writer reports the sentiments of the multitude, it is obvious that she does not share them. She reveals her *irony* (a figure of speech in which the words used convey the opposite of their literal meaning) in the belittling comparison of Hesperus with rocket light and in the final unimaginative question.
7. Have you ever been at the seashore at night? What was there to see, to hear, to feel, to smell? What visions, what emotions, what thoughts came over you?
8. Notice the rhyme scheme and the stanza pattern. What do they contribute to the poem?
9. These words are worth knowing:
    a. twink (line 4)
    b. twirl (line 4)
    c. comets (line 5)
    d. purl (line 5)
    e. strand (line 7)

Afterword

You have now completed what is, in essence, a primer of poetry. It is the writer's hope that you have gained the insight, skill and confidence necessary to read increasingly difficult and demanding—and increasingly rewarding—poetry of all kinds.

Many of the author's former students have discovered the delight of writing, as well as reading, verse. Perhaps you, too, will someday attempt to express your strongest emotions and profoundest thoughts in this way. These two arts, both the reading and writing of poetry, serve the same end: they broaden, deepen and heighten the joy of living.